Abe Builds a Birdhouse

A Book about Animal Homes

BY KERRY DINMONT

Published by The Child's World®
1980 Lookout Drive • Mankato, MN 56003-1705
800-599-READ • www.childsworld.com

Photographs ©: Anna Sedneva/Shutterstock Images, cover, 1 (top), 3;
Shutterstock Images, 1 (bottom), 5, 9, 13, 18 (middle), 21; Steve Cole
Images/iStockphoto, 6; Oliver Hoffmann/Shutterstock Images, 10; Cindy
Underwood/Shutterstock Images, 14; iStockphoto, 17; Eric Isselee/
Shutterstock Images, 18 (top); Steve Byland/Shutterstock Images, 18
(bottom)

Design Elements: Shutterstock Images

ISBN 9781503820166
LCCN 2016960934

Printed in the United States of America
PA02339

Today, Abe builds a birdhouse.

Why is he building it?

6

Abe and his dad build
a birdhouse. It will be
a home for **wild** birds.

The birdhouse is made of wood. Many birds like wood homes. They nest in trees or wood fences.

The birdhouse has a
roof. The roof keeps
the inside dry.

There is a hole in one wall. Birds will use the hole to get in and out.

Birds will build a nest
inside. They will lay eggs.

Chicks will **hatch** from the eggs. The birdhouse keeps them warm and dry.

17

Abe hangs the birdhouse in a tree. What bird will live here?

How would you build

a birdhouse?

Words to Know

hatch (HACH) To hatch is to break out of an egg. Baby birds hatch out of eggs.

wild (WILD) To be wild is to live in natural conditions and not be controlled by or cared for by humans. Wild birds live in nature and are not pets.

Extended Learning Activities

1 If you built a birdhouse, where would you hang it?

2 Have you ever seen a bird's nest? Where was it?

3 What do you think birds use to build their nests?

To Learn More

Books

Alderfer, Jonathan K. *National Geographic Kids Bird Guide of North America: The Best Birding Book for Kids from National Geographic's Bird Experts*. Washington, DC: National Geographic, 2013.

Miller, Mirella S. *Build a Birdhouse*. Mankato, MN: The Child's World, 2017.

Web Sites

Visit our Web site for links about birdhouses:
childsworld.com/links

Note to Parents, Teachers, and Librarians: We routinely verify our Web links to make sure they are safe and active sites. So encourage your readers to check them out!

About the Author

Kerry Dinmont is a children's book author who enjoys art and nature. She lives in Montana with her two Norwegian elkhounds.